LOGICAL FALLACIES
an introduction for children

Written and illustrated by

BEVERLY PEARL

For Stephan, André and Nick

☺ Attribution Share-Alike

Production: H&S Le Temps H&S Times
http://www.tempshstimes.com/

ISBN : 978-1-927974-32-2

Contents

Synopsis

Danny finds an abandoned baby crow and takes care of it. The crow now attached to Danny, follows him to school every day. The other students jokingly refer to the crow as "Danny's Dog". Logical Fallacies begin to unfold when a bully pushes Danny down. Through a variety of logically fallacious exchanges, Danny is blamed and punished for starting the fight. During a second encounter with the bully, "Danny Dog" catches the attention of a teacher with his loud cawing, in time for her to see the lie unfold. The teacher decides to teach the children about what logical fallacies are and how to spot them. The story presented as a poem that shares the experiences of the fictional Grove St. School children as they learn about logical fallacies. Illustration include speech bubbles representing some of the fallacies as they may manifest among school children.

Forward

The same fallacious discussion and bullying that is found in the school yard can often be found within upper management and around board room tables. It is hoped that introducing these concepts early will help contribute to the emotional intelligence of children and ultimately a more enlightened leadership in governments and organizations. A knowledgeable population might not be easy to gaslight if they are empowered to trust their own instincts, acknowledge nuance and think for themselves.

Definition of a 'Fallacy'

"A misconception resulting from a flaw in reasoning, or a trick or illusion in thoughts, that often succeeds in obfuscating facts/truth."
From: Logical Fallacies, **https://www.logicalfallacies.org/**

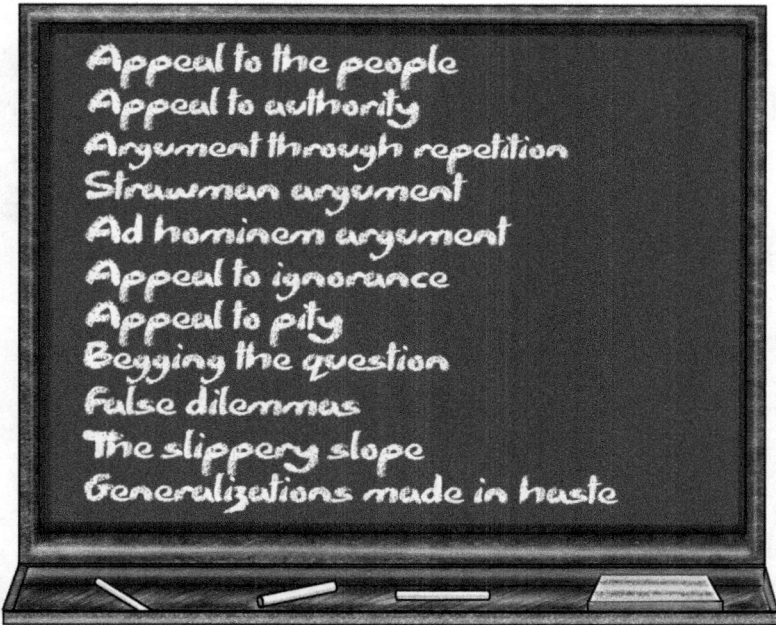

"We know it was you."

Chapter 1

Learning to ask

This is how at Grove-Street school the children learned to ask,

questions that would would help them see the truth in any task.

Is it helpful to repeat the things that someone says

or to believe what someone claims because your classmate does?

Sometimes things can look one way depending on your stance,

but they can look quite different if you take another glance.

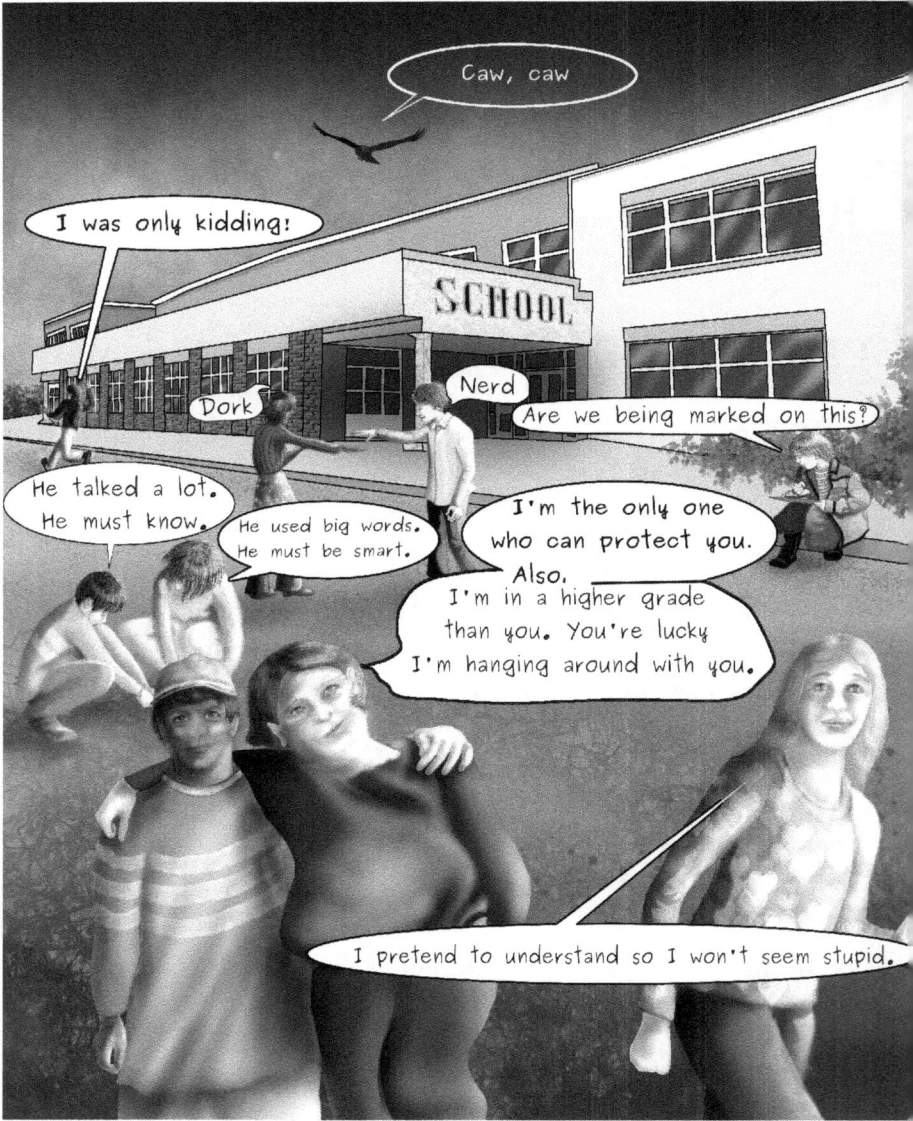

Chapter 2

Danny finds a crow

Danny found a baby crow, beneath a Grove-Street tree,

brought it in the house to feed, then to set it free.

All through summer baby grew and quickly learned to fly,

but when autumn came the crow just wouldn't say goodbye.

It followed Dan to school each day, even in the fog.

The other kids would joke around. They called it "Danny's-Dog."

"I will take care of you."

Chapter 3

Dan's bully

Once a bully pushed our Dan, right into the muck.

"He hit first!" the bully bawled. "I could barely duck!"

Other children gathered round as Danny brushed his clothes.

"He hit first!" they chanted too. "Everybody knows!"

Caw, caw caw, said Danny's-Dog, circling above.

Then a teacher asked to know who was first to shove.

Chapter 4

Ganging up

"Dan hit first." the children said, and slowly backed away.

(Danny's-Dog from Grove St. cawed, but really couldn't say.)

Danny had detention, then. That was very bad.

Teacher sent a note home too, to tell his mom and dad.

Dirty clothes, accusing friends, didn't look too good.

All believed the bully's lie. Anybody would.

Dan in detention.

Chapter 5

Fallout

Parents lectured Danny, too. "Children shouldn't fight!"

Danny tried to tell the truth, but "Teacher must be right!"

Punishment at home was swift - grounded for a week.

Danny felt so lonely, and confused, and sad and bleak.

Next day at school the children said, "You must apologize."

Danny's-Dog cried "Caw! Caw! No!", while circling in the skies.

Chapter 6

That bully again

Again, the bully hit our Dan. "Apologize!" they said.

"and stop your stupid crow or we will shut him up instead."

Bully pushed again and cried, "You must stop pushing me!"

This time, on patrol, a teacher near them got to see.

Danny's-Dog made such a noise that teacher saw it all.

Danny's-Dog and teacher both had seen our Danny fall.

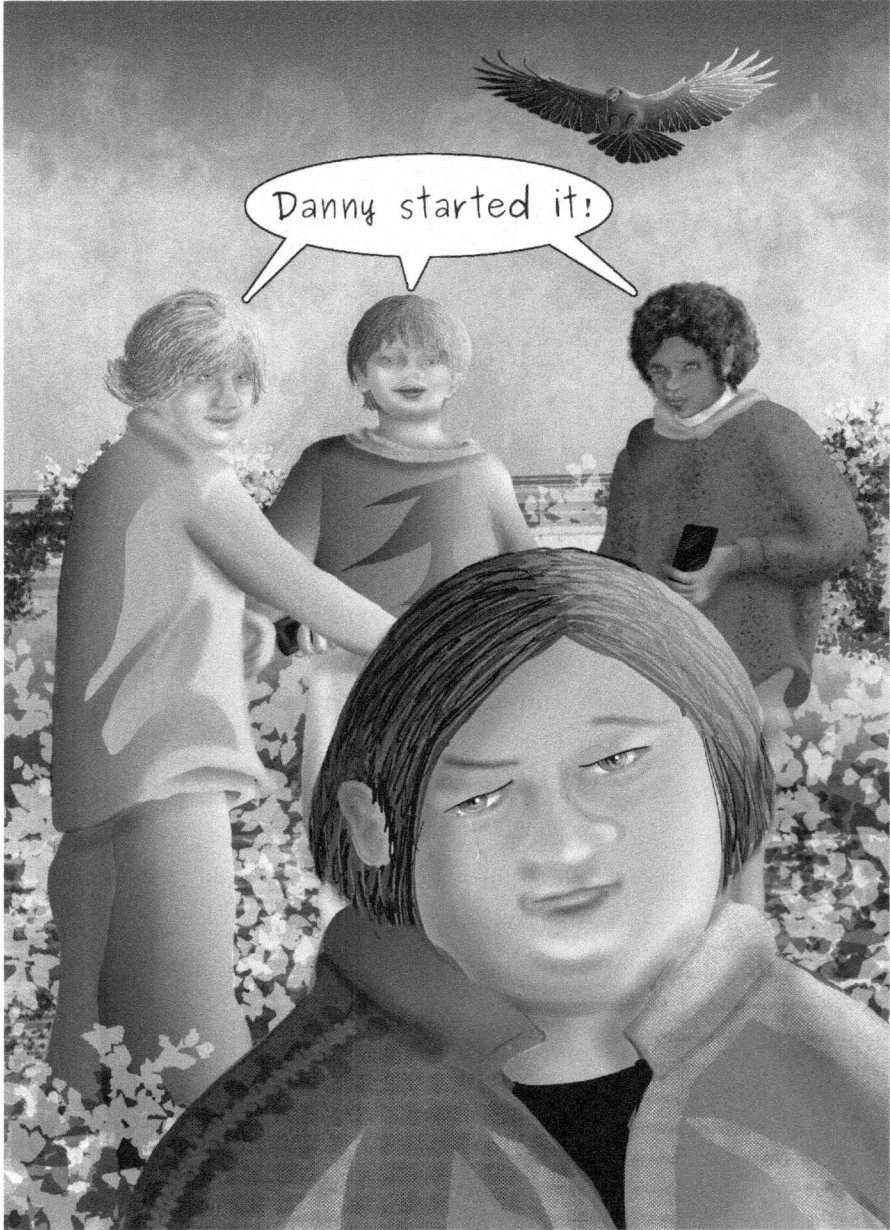

Chapter 7

The intervention

"Danny started it!" again the angry bully cried.

"Danny started it!" said all the children at his side.

Teacher knew this wasn't true and now there was some doubt

if the children even knew what this was all about.

"Come with me," the teacher said. "Come, and come right now."

"We can sort things like this out. I will show you how."

Chapter 8

The lesson begins

In the classroom, teacher wrote some words upon the board.

"These are types of arguments we really can't afford:

"Appeal to people," That is one. "Authority" is two.

"These fallacies have come to mind when listening to you.

"At first the group believed a lie. Then a teacher too.

"The teacher, the authority, told parents what he knew."

Chapter 9

How lies are believed

"Repetition" is another method to deceive.

Repeating blame was what had caused the students to believe.

If everyone believes a lie, that doesn't make it true.

One teacher just accepted, though, that everybody knew.

The parents thought the teacher was the boss, and so must know.

The only ones who told the truth were Danny and his crow.

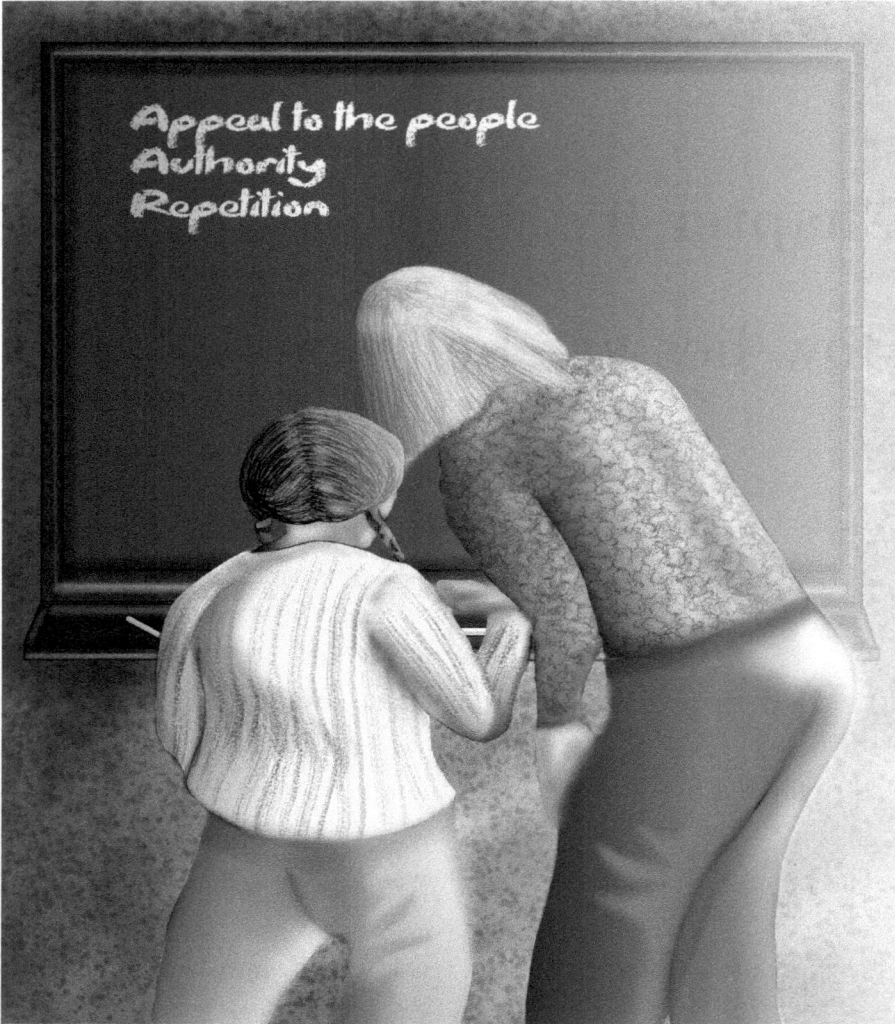

Chapter 10

Lots of ways to lie

False arguments like these are often used to ill effect,

and it can cause some trouble if your sources go un-checked.

Fallacies are commonplace, and these are only three.

So let's explore a couple more that now occur to me.

"Straw-man" is a claim that's made, but just to knock it down.

"False equivalence" can be enough to make you frown.

Chapter 11

So many logical fallacies!

"Ad Hominem" or "Ignorance", "Appeal to pity" too

"Red herring" or a "The bandwagon", are ones we should eschew.

"Cum Hoc, Ergo Propter Hoc", or "False analogy",

"Appeal to our ignorance" is common fallacy.

"Beg the question", "False dilemmas", and "The slippery slope",

And "Generalizations made in haste", won't be used, I hope.

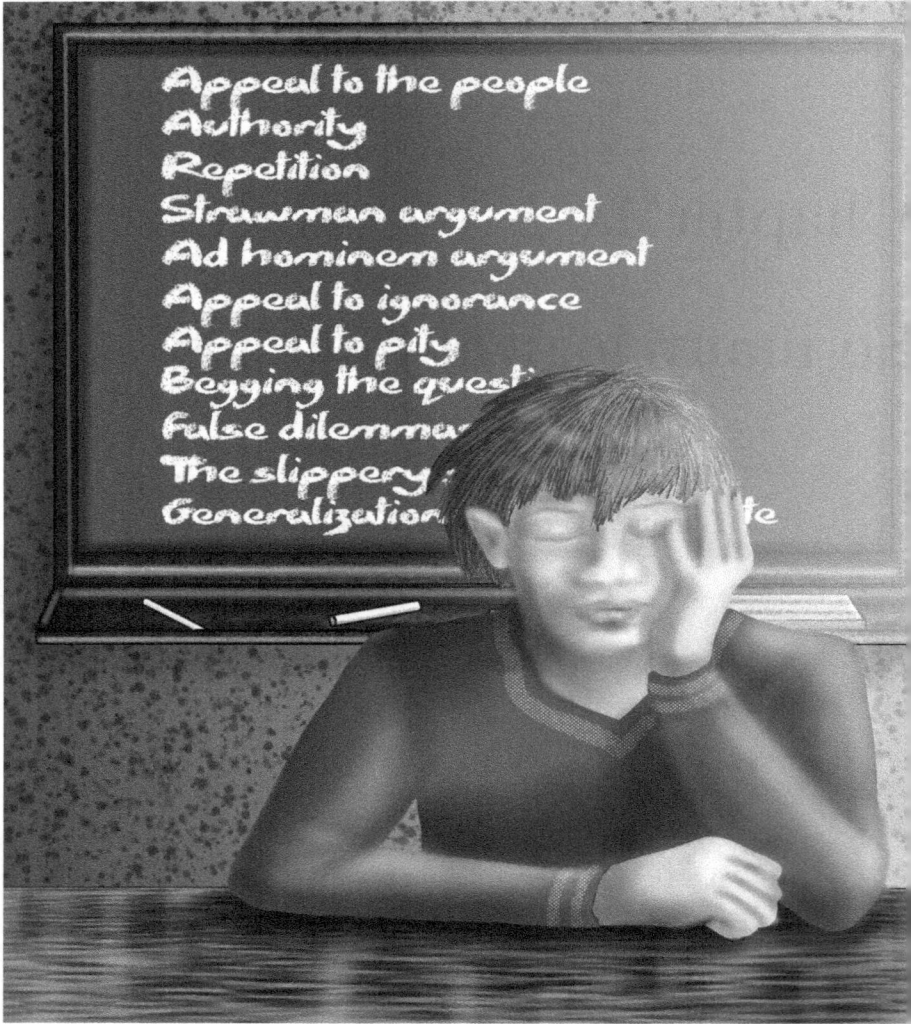

Chapter 12

Lesson learned

There are also many other ways to twist the truth.

Knowing them can help us each become a better sleuth.

Danny isn't bullied now, and reason is the rule.

"How to question" is a formal lesson in his school.

Now these students check their facts, avoiding mental fog.

They learned how to seek the truth, because of Danny's-Dog.

Chapter 13

Definitions

- **Appeal to the People (Argumentum ad Populum):** This fallacy presumes that something is true if many people believe it.

Example : All the children said that Danny started the fight, so the teacher who came to investigate believed it to be true.

- **Appeal to authority:** If someone who should know what they are talking about believes something, it must be true.

Example : A teacher believed that Danny started the fight, so his parents also believed it.

- **Argument from Repetition:** Repeating something is a powerful way to make people believe it, but that doesn't make it true.

Example : Kids kept repeating that Danny started the fight when he didn't.

- **Straw-man arguments:** This is the misrepresentation of an argument so that it becomes easier to attack – setting up a "straw-man" in order to knock it down instead of addressing the actual argument.

<u>Example :</u> The bully blamed Danny's crow for annoying him to deflect from his own guilt.

- **Ad hominem argument:** An ad hominem attack takes place when the arguer tries to undermine an argument using personal attacks.

<u>Example :</u> Danny says he didn't do it but students think he is a liar, so they can't trust his word .

- **Appeal to Ignorance:** Appeal to Ignorance states that a statement must be true if it cannot be proven false.

<u>Example :</u> We couldn't figure out why the air moved when there was no window open, so it must have been a ghost.

- **Appeal to pity:** A claim is made based on emotion rather than logic.

<u>Example :</u> The bully told Danny that their kitten died before demanding an apology. The possible death of a kitten has nothing to do with whether or not Danny should apologize for something he hasn't done.

- **Begging the question:** Begging the question is when an argument's premise assumes a conclusion.

<u>Example :</u> One would be begging the question if one said, "So, Danny, when you hit the bully how does it feel?"

- **The False Dilemma:** This fallacy presents complex issues in simple, opposing terms. It assumes that there can be only two outcomes. Usually one of the outcomes is better than the other, which encourages one to select the better one despite its fallacious roots.

Example : Danny is given a choice between being punished for something he hasn't done or apologizing for something he hasn't done.

- **The slippery slope:** Slippery slope arguments reason that thing A will lead to thing B and so should be avoided.

Example : If we let Danny's crow follow him to school, it might fly up to the roof where it could eventually get caught in a ventilation fan.

- **Generalizations made in haste:** This fallacy is about jumping to conclusions without any evidence to support a claim.

Example : Everyone said that Danny started the fight, though no one had seen it happen.

- **Proof by Verbosity:** Also called argumentum verbosium or proof by intimidation, this argument is too complicated and verbose for the listener to address the contents.

Example : "A corvus* can't possibly understand the nuance of human altercation, which obfuscates our conclusions about the whole encounter." *crow

- **Red Herring:** The red herring focuses on an irrelevant topic so as to distract the listener, either to deflect or to focus on a subject that the speaker knows well.

Example : "Maybe I did push Danny first, but his stupid crow annoys me."

27

- **Cum Hoc, ergo propter hoc:** This is Latin for "with this therefore because of this." It is sometimes described as correlation vs causation. It suggests that two things happening at the same time have a causal relationship.

Example : Danny's crow cawed when the bully was pushing Dan, therefore the crow must have caused the bully to push Dan.

"One of the first things you learn in any statistics class is that correlation doesn't imply causation. Nonetheless, it's fun to consider the causal relationships one could infer from these correlations." ~~
Ky Harlin, (when referring to bizarre correlations.)[1]

- **Gaslighting:** "A form of psychological manipulation in which a person or a group covertly sows seeds of doubt in a targeted individual or group, making them question their own memory perception, or judgement." ~~ Wikipedia [2]

Example : Everyone who told Danny that he was lying when he said he did not start the fight was gaslighting him.

---

[1]Harlin, Ky, Director of Data Science. "The 10 Most Bizarre Correlations." *Buzzfeed.* 11 April 2013. Retrieved from **https://www.buzzfeednews.com/article/kjh2110/the-10-most-bizarre-correlations**
[2]"*Gaslighting.*" Wikipedia.
Retrieved from: **https://en.wikipedia.org/wiki/Gaslighting**

Citations

"Logical Fallacies." *Logical Fallacies.*
Retrieved from: **https://www.logicalfallacies.org/**

Cook, Carla. "15 Common Logical Fallacies
and How to Spot Them."
Hubspot. 27 April 2021. Retrieved from:
**https://blog.hubspot.com/
marketing/common-logical-fallacies**

Virgen, Tyler. "Spurious Correlations." *tylervirgen.com.*
Retrieved from:
https://tylervigen.com/spurious-correlations

For a larger list of fallacies: "List of Fallacies.
" *Wikipedia.* 13 June 2021. Retrieved from:
https://en.wikipedia.org/wiki/List_of_fallacies

If any of these links are dead, a saved copy
can be retrieved from the Internet Archive's Wayback Machine
at: **https://web.archive.org**

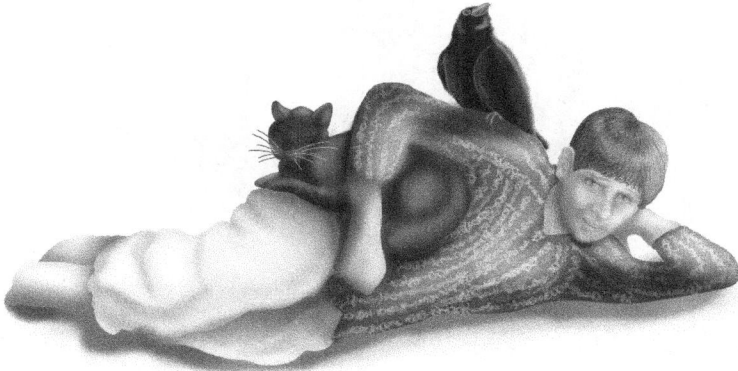

Chapter 14

Noticing

How many logical fallacies can you find in the following pictures, and
what are they called?

What would you do instead?

Group-think.

"Come with me and come right now."